No Rouz
Our Persian New Year

E. S. Zameen

Author's Note: Persian words do not have a standardized spelling in English. In this book I have chosen spellings that are phonetically accurate and, I hope, the most accessible and intuitive. Syllables are hyphenated, and h's are used to attain the familiar "ah" and "eh" vowel pronunciation. This, in hopes of making your experience here most enjoyable.

May the beauty of No Rouz
Be a delight to your soul,
ESZ

For my family, and with special thanks to my editor.

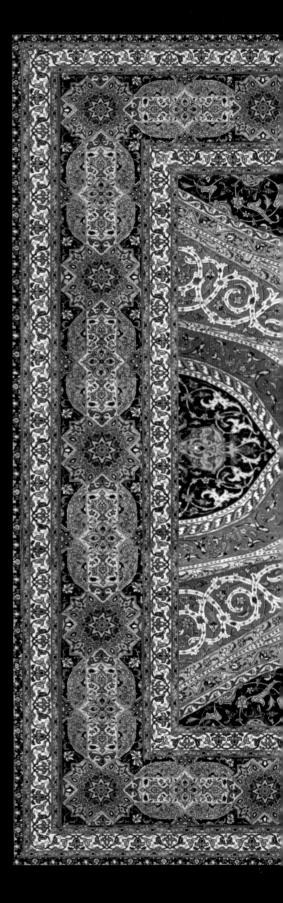

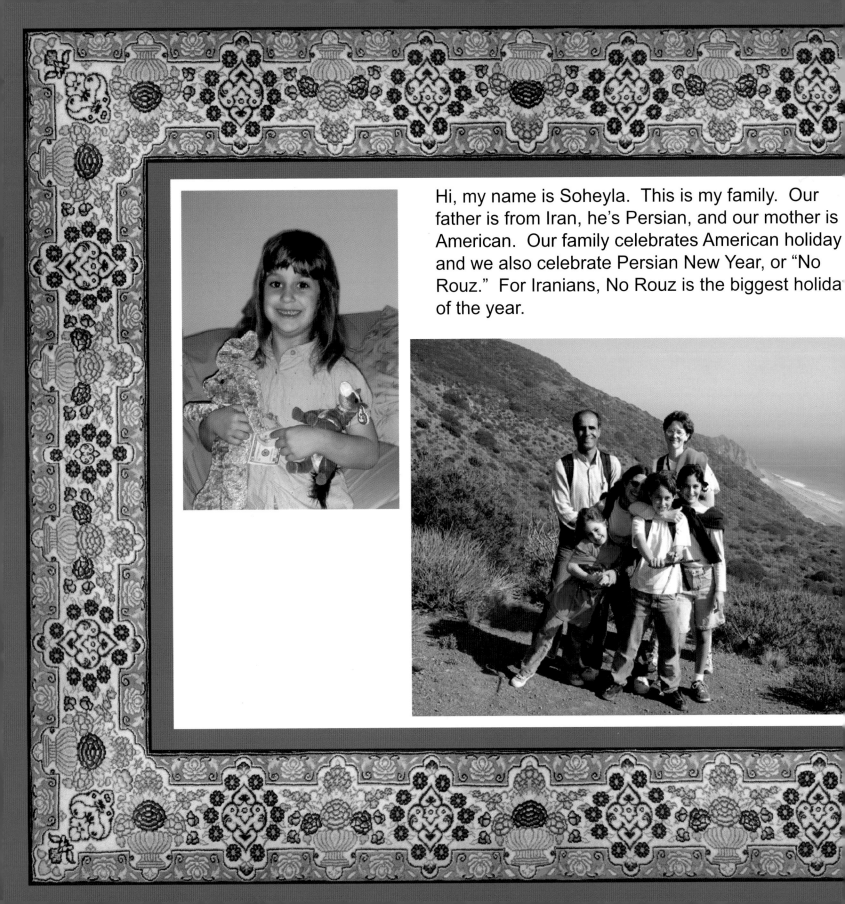

Hi, my name is Soheyla. This is my family. Our father is from Iran, he's Persian, and our mother is American. Our family celebrates American holiday and we also celebrate Persian New Year, or "No Rouz." For Iranians, No Rouz is the biggest holida of the year.

When the month of March comes, it is time to get ready for No Rouz. The New Year always starts on the first day of Spring, which is on or near March 21. The first thing we do is to grow some sprouts. They are called "sabzeh." Sabzeh represent new life and the earth turning green at springtime.

We spray them with water several times a day, and soon they begin to sprout.

Traditionally, it is believed that as the sabzeh grow, they absorb any bad feelings in the home. (You will see what we do with them!)

row the sprouts, first we soak overnight. Then we drain them put them on a plate.

We also prepare for No Rouz by cleaning our house. We all help. It is our biggest cleaning of the year, to make everything new and bright again.

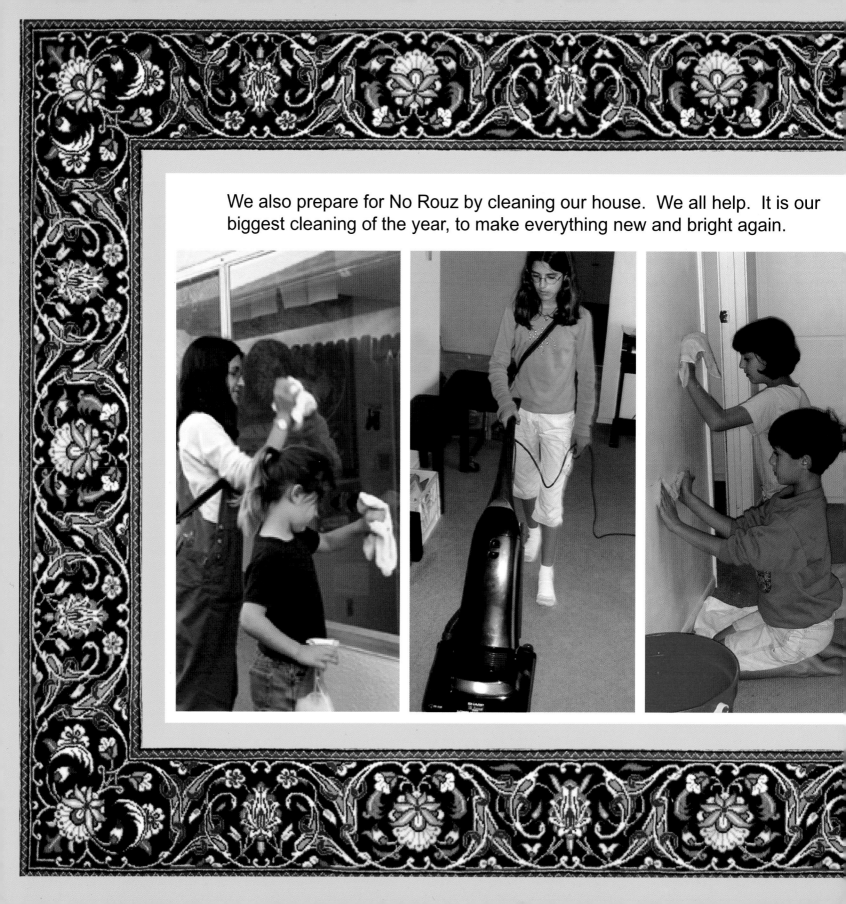

It takes us all week. Whew, it feels good when we are done!

We also go shopping for new clothes and new shoes.

It's all part of starting the year fresh and new.

There are some things we need for No Rouz that aren't in the regular stores. Sinc we're not far from Los Angeles, mom goes to the specialty stores there. In some parts of the city, the signs are in Persian.

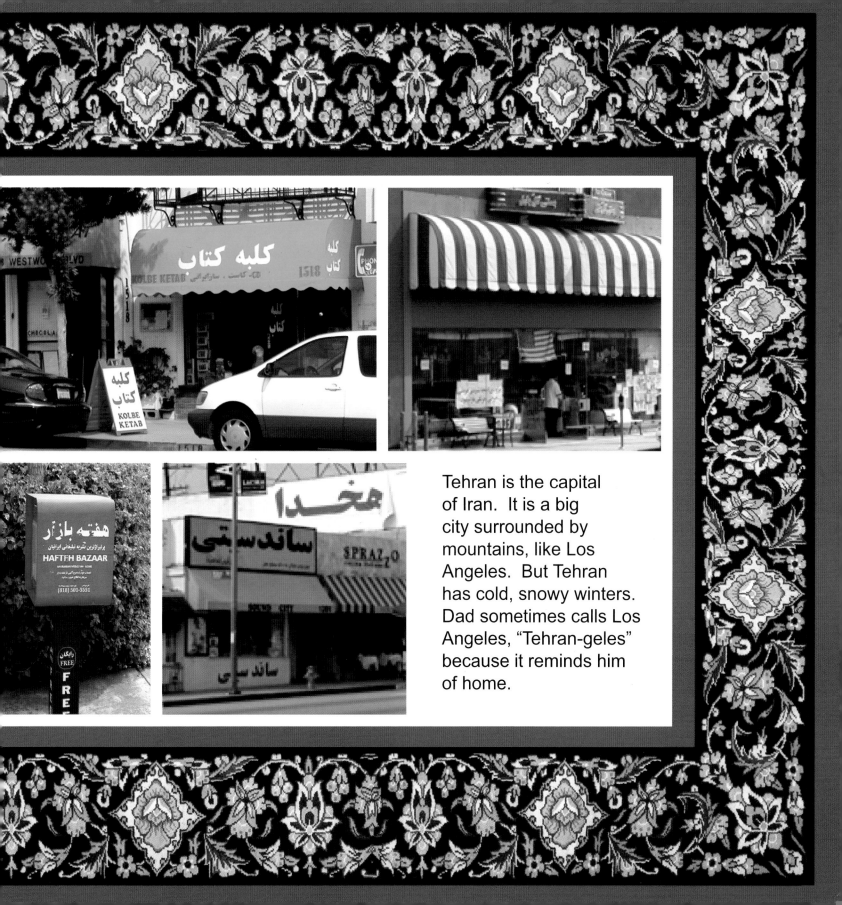

Tehran is the capital of Iran. It is a big city surrounded by mountains, like Los Angeles. But Tehran has cold, snowy winters. Dad sometimes calls Los Angeles, "Tehran-geles" because it reminds him of home.

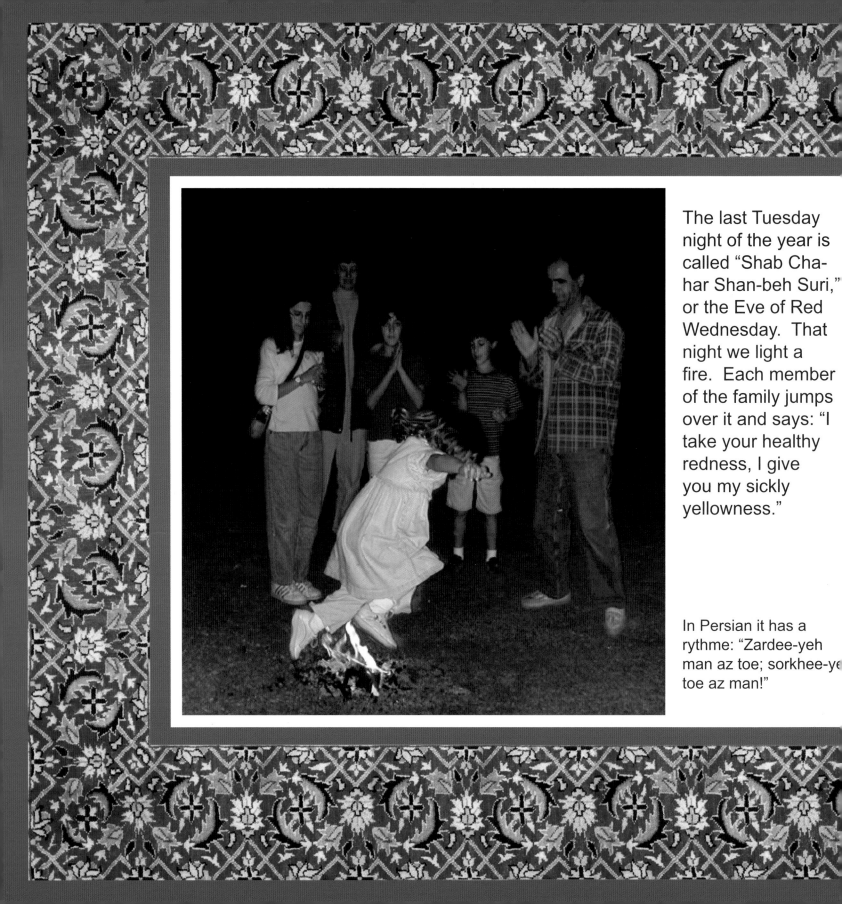

The last Tuesday night of the year is called "Shab Cha-har Shan-beh Suri," or the Eve of Red Wednesday. That night we light a fire. Each member of the family jumps over it and says: "I take your healthy redness, I give you my sickly yellowness."

In Persian it has a rythme: "Zardee-yeh man az toe; sorkhee-ye toe az man!"

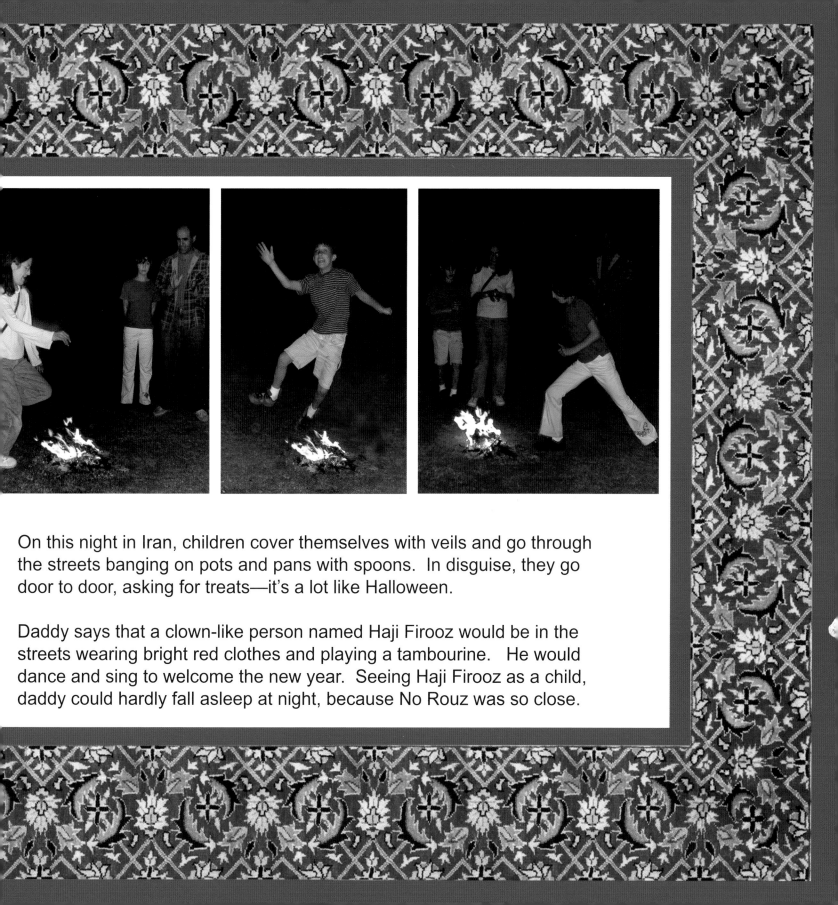

On this night in Iran, children cover themselves with veils and go through the streets banging on pots and pans with spoons. In disguise, they go door to door, asking for treats—it's a lot like Halloween.

Daddy says that a clown-like person named Haji Firooz would be in the streets wearing bright red clothes and playing a tambourine. He would dance and sing to welcome the new year. Seeing Haji Firooz as a child, daddy could hardly fall asleep at night, because No Rouz was so close.

Our sprouts are tall now and No Rouz is almost here. We put a red ribbon around our sabzeh and prepare a special table called "So-freh-yeh Haft Seen." This means the tablecloth of seven S's. There are seven things on the table that start with the Persian letter S. They are:

1. Sabzeh - sprouts
2. Seeb - an apple
3. Sumac - a sour spice
4. Seer - garlic

5. Sohan - a pistachio cookie
6. Senjed - a fruit of the lotus tree
7. Sehkeh - coins

There are other things on the table too: a mirror, candles, colored eggs, water, and goldfish. Each thing on the table represents something good for the coming year — new life, health, prosperity, and happiness.

Actually, there are other S things we could use: serkeh (vinegar) or samanu (a kind of pudding). The Haft Seen can have different things, depending on a family's traditions.

This is the day of No Rouz. The new year starts at the moment of the Spring equinox—so it can be any time of the day. We sit together on the couch. Daddy hugs each of us and wishes us a good year. He also gives us money. We call our Persian relatives and say, "Aid-eh Sho-mah Mo-bar-ak!" to wish them a happy new year.

Pastries, nuts and fruit are always nearby during No Rouz. I love the sweet pastries. Mmm, mmm!

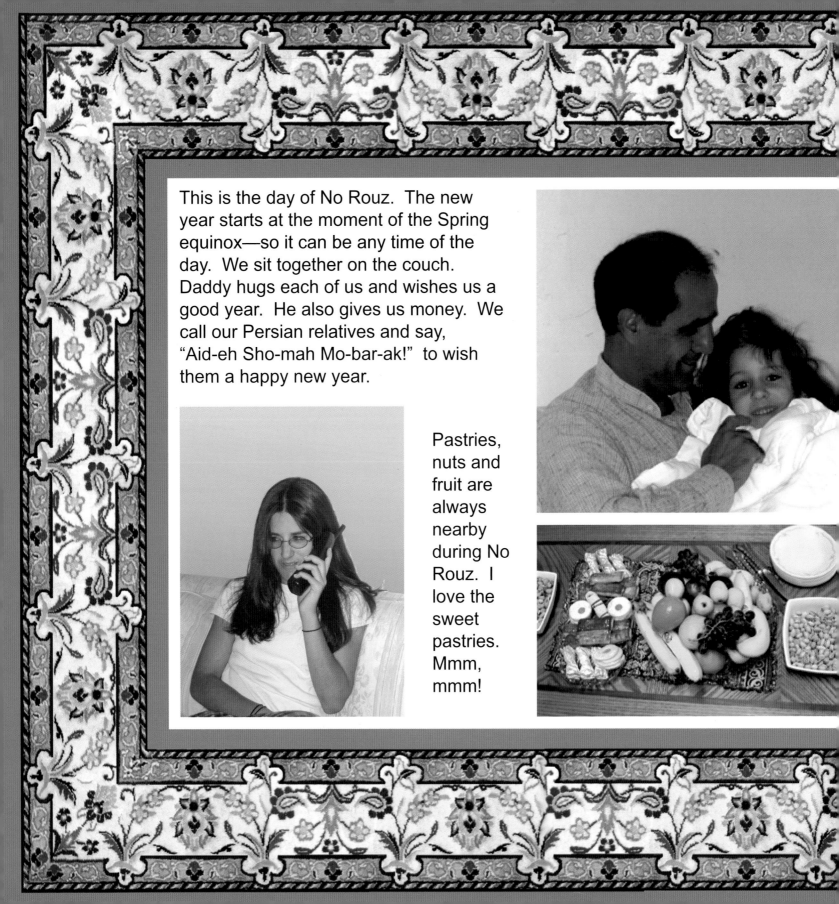

The gift money is called "Ay Dee." Dad always gives crisp, new bills.

The New Year meal is a big part of No Rouz. Mom cooks for a lor time. It is a lot like Thanksgiving, only with Persian food. We have rice, fish, noodle soup, bread and feta cheese, cucumber yogurt, an "kookoo" which is like a pancake made of vegetables and eggs.

The food is wonderful. My favorite is the bread and feta cheese. It is nice to be together. We talk about last year and laugh about the funny things that happened.

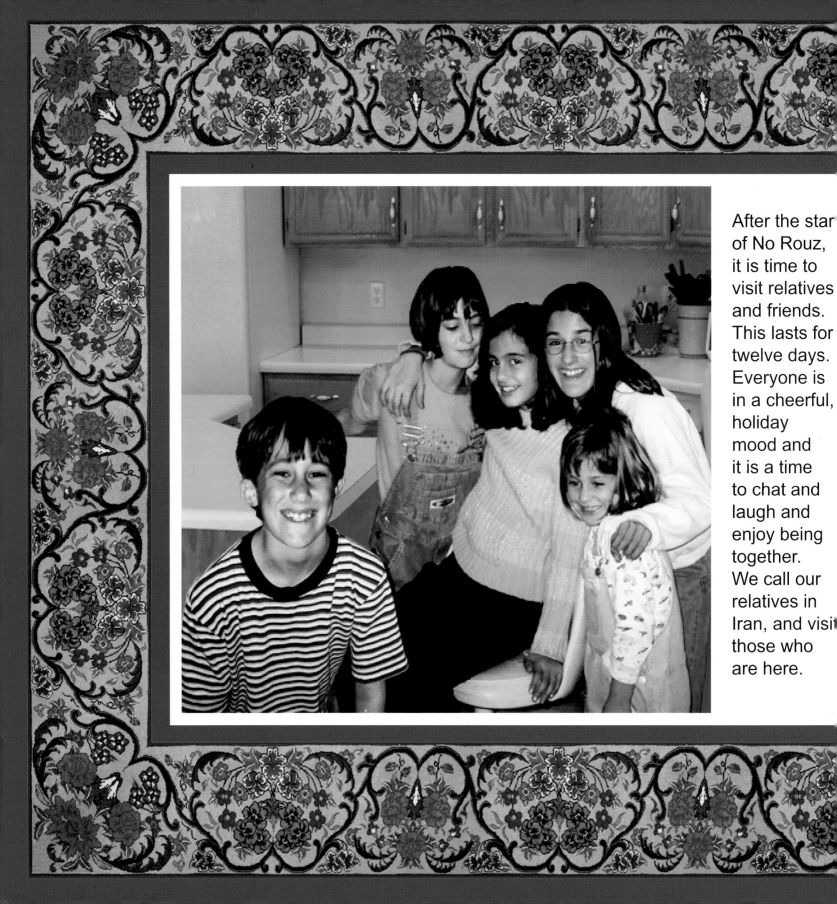

After the star of No Rouz, it is time to visit relatives and friends. This lasts for twelve days. Everyone is in a cheerful, holiday mood and it is a time to chat and laugh and enjoy being together. We call our relatives in Iran, and visit those who are here.

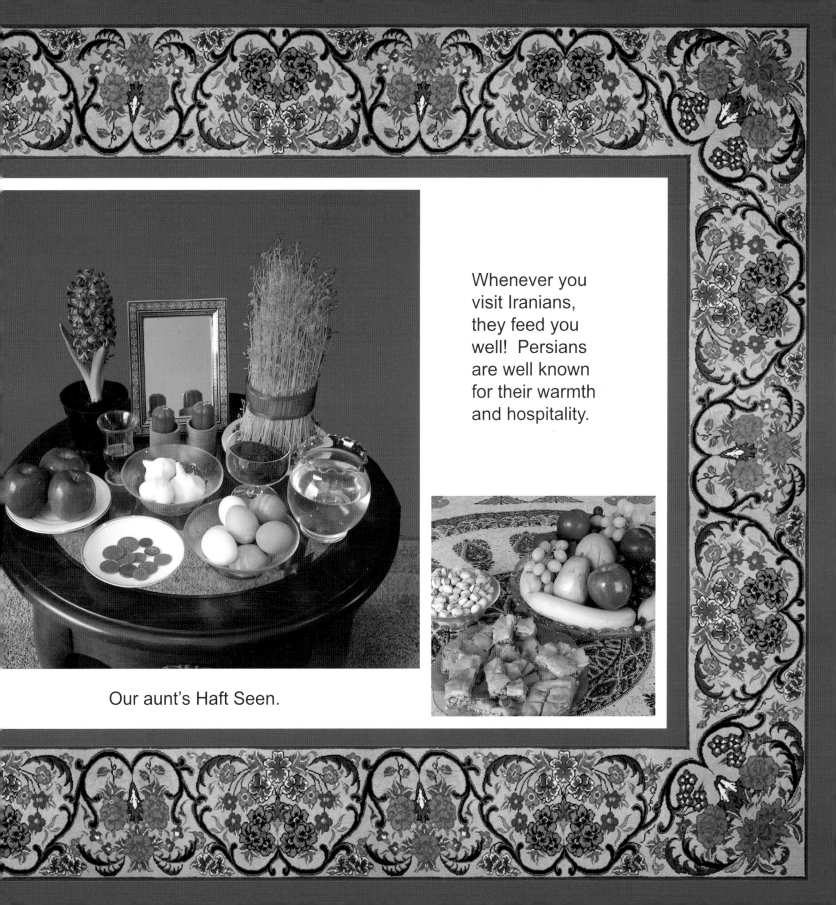

Whenever you visit Iranians, they feed you well! Persians are well known for their warmth and hospitality.

Our aunt's Haft Seen.

We go visit Iranian friends in Los Angeles. They also give us Ay Dee.

Persian goodbyes can last a while!

The thirteenth day of the year is a fun day. It is called "Seez-deh Beh-dar", which means "throw out the thirteenth." It is unlucky to stay indoors. Everyone goes out to a park or the countryside for a picnic and to enjoy the day.

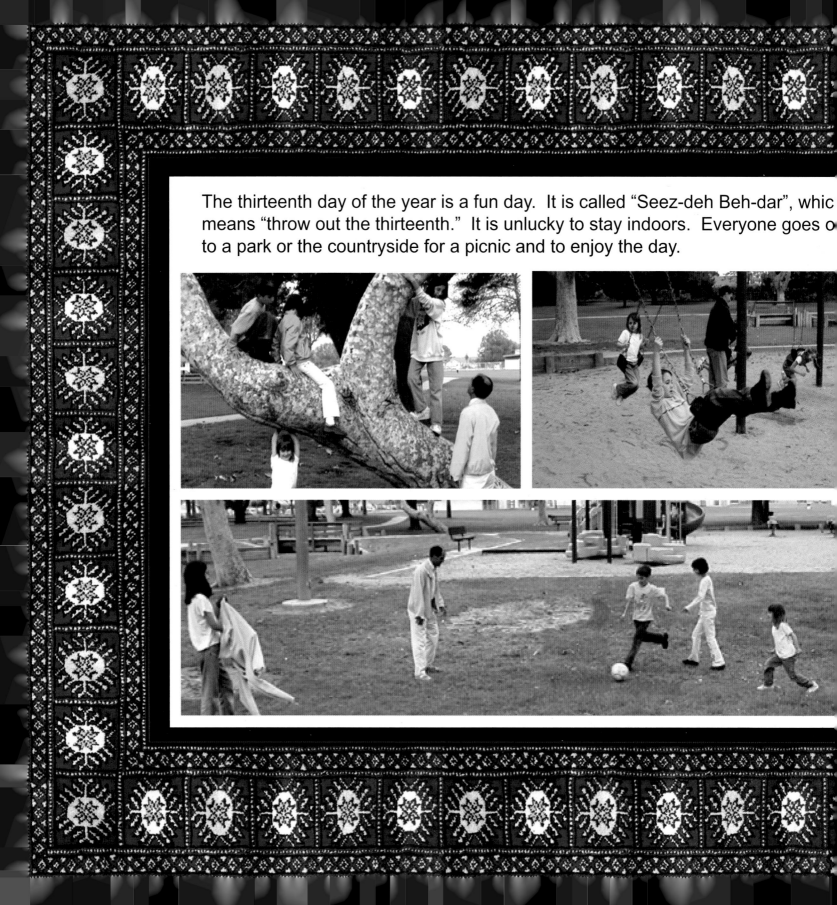

We'll have rice with lima beans and dill, barbequed chicken, pita bread, cucumber yogurt, salad, fried eggplant, fresh greens and radishes, and "tadeek"– the crunchy rice from the bottom of the pan. We *all* love tadeek.

Strawberry shortcake with whip cream–yum! American dessert is fine with me!

Before we come home from our picnic, we throw our sabzeh into a stream of running water. By doing this, we throw away all the family's troubles from last year. This way, the new year begins fresh and new.

The park is not far from the beach, and the stream takes our sabzeh out into the wide, beautiful ocean. Goodbye, old year!   Welcome, new year! Aid-eh Sho-mah Moe-bah-rak!

More things to know about
the country, culture,
and language . . .

Iran and its People

Iran is in the middle east. As you can see, Iran has many neighbors.   Most Iranians are Persian. In many of Iran's neighboring countries, people are Arab. Iran's capital is Tehran, a city of 14 million people. The population of Iran is about 68 million.

No Rouz (or variations of No Rouz) are also celebrated in Pakistan, Iraq, Afghanistan and other nearby countries.

The United States census in the year 2000 found that there were 338,000 people of Iranian ancestry living in the United States.

Persian Food

Food is a *very* important part of Persian culture. In general, Persian cuisine is sour. Iranians use fresh or dried lemon in many dishes. Dinner often consists of rice with a sauce or stew on top, herbs, salad, and plain yogurt. For dessert, Persians usually eat fruit, or sometimes sweets, which are often flavored with pistachios and rose water.   Here is an easy recipe you can try.

Cucumber Yogurt with Bread

1½ cups plain yogurt
½ of a medium cucumber
½ of a small clove of garlic (optional)
¼ teaspoon salt
a dash of pepper
pita bread or other bread

Peel the cucumber, then grate it onto a cutting board. Chop the grated cucumber a bit so the pieces are smaller. Put the yogurt in a medium size bowl and add the cucumber. If desired, mince the garlic and add to the bowl. Add salt and pepper, then stir it all up. (Taste it and see if it needs more salt.)

Toast a circle of pita bread, then cut it into 6 triangles (like how you cut pizza). Spoon the cucumber yogurt onto a warm wedge of pita bread. Enjoy!

Persian Language

Persian is also called Farsi. Persian is written from right to left–the opposite of English. So, the back of a book in English would be the front of a Persian book. The alphabet has 32 letters. Here are some things you can say and write in Persian:

English	Persian	Persian
Hello.	Saläm.	سلام
How are you?	Chetoree?	چطوری
Fine, thank you.	Khoobam, mamnoon.	خوبم ممنون
Goodbye.	Khodä hafez.	خداحافظ

How to say the sounds:
  "Kh" is a grating, grinding sound deep in the throat.
  "a" = a like in cat
  "ä" = a like in father

Persian and Arabic are different languages that use the same alphabet–just like English and Spanish use the same alphabet.

More Resources

No Rouz
These web sites are about No Rouz. You can also search them for information about Iran's history and current events.

FarsiNet
http://www.farsinet.com/norooz/

Norooz International Cultural Foundation
http://www.norooz.ca/index.html

Iranian Cultural Information Center
http://persia.org/

Wikipedia
http://en.wikipedia.org/wiki/Norouz

Iran Chamber Society
http://www.iranchamber.com/culture/articles/norooz_iranian_new_year.php

The Odyssey: World Trek for Service & Education
http://www.worldtrek.org/odyssey/mideast/040100/040100kavinoruz.html

Recipes
In A Persian Kitchen by Maideh Mazda.

Persian Rugs
Did you notice the Persian rugs on the borders of this book? Most of these beautiful pictures came from Adib's Rug Gallery. Adib's, and many others, have information about Persian rugs on their web sites.